INTROSPECTIONS

and
consequential
poems

Paul Dignan

A Square One Publication

First published by
Square One Publications
Sansome Place, Worcester WR1 1RU

ISBN: 1 872017 59 2

British Library Cataloguing-in-Publication Data.
A catalogue record for this book is available from the British Library.

Typeset by Brightset, Brighton
in Plantin 12/15

Printed in Great Britain by Antony Rowe Ltd

INTROSPECTIONS

NO ES EL TIEMPO
QUE PASA
SINO
NOSOTROS QUE PASAMOS

Previous Volumes
by same author
and publisher

XLIMMIQX (1990)

THE END OF THE WORLD (1991)

CONTENTS

INTRODUCTIONS

"... NOCTURNAL INTROIT"

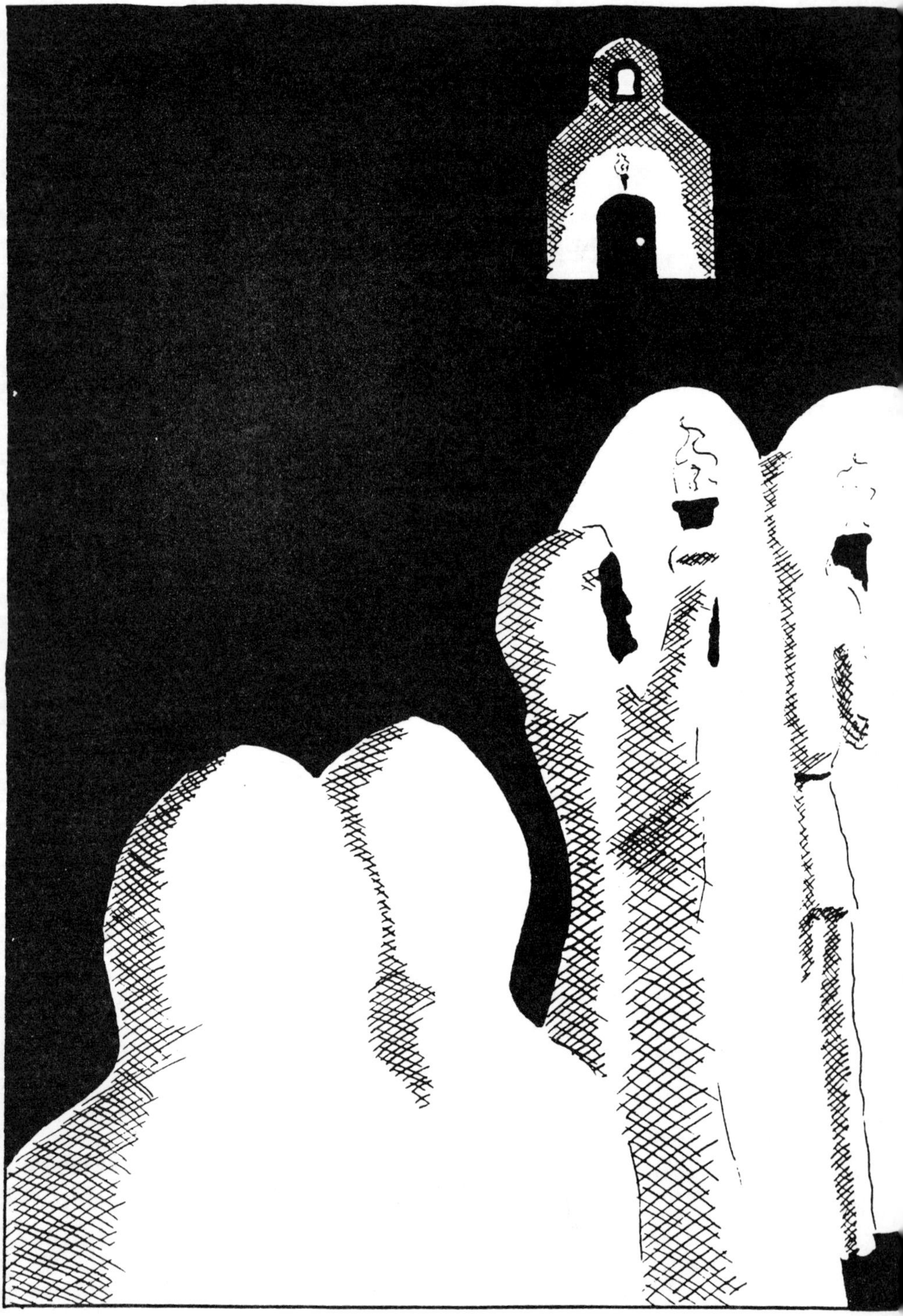

INTROSPECTIONS

The words are just
beyond the reach
of those unwise
enough to sleep

Innominate
syllabic doubt
intensifies
displacement

and pattern projects
are progressively
intended as
a counterpart

The extra special
obstinacy
of most objects
inanimate

relevant
resilience
behaviour motion
mechanistic

preclude adversely
in several ways
the opposite
destructively

Relinquishment
of incantation
will overcome
the unavoid

an atrophy
of atavistic
olden orders
past redemption

the antonym
of understanding
does not revive
the trilogism

nocturnal introit
was the meaning
last no longer
saving gracious

There being
no advantage
nor disadvantage
in diffusion

summation is
to recommence
addictively
half insecure

responsive new
each indistinction
extended by
postponement

the words again
are just beyond
the reach of those
still sleeping

the attribute
amazement more
and afterwards
were found before.

ELIPSES

"... WATCHING FROM AFAR"

Search forsaken I stand aloof
becoming more and more detached
from life and from society
as though I were not here
but watching from afar
displaced by distance
positioned on a mountain
clear horizon wide
to hear yet be not heard
to see myself unseen
the great impossibilities
whence everything
is happening repetitiously
and simultaneous together
merged overwrought
in everywhere enough
as when I stand apart
becoming more detached
to see the whole entirety
of seven thousand years
rolled back upon themselves
to where had not then yet begun
the sequences of centuries to run.

Though I were somewhile there
a separate way of life
yet I am here
to know what could have been
if there were any choice
to live in different times
and other places
by circumstance restricted
to be myself as someone else
but still the same as me
and by my forbears fashioned
when all of us are here
and I am now
as from myself descended.

A picture of the past is clear
   in sleep unbroken;

distorted images appear
   as we are woken
by words we indistinctly hear
that rapidly evaporate
   as soon as spoken;

the consequences we await;

   what they betoken
collective memories collate.

In nightmares I have seen them
thinking they do not exist
save in the minds
of their conceivers
close confined
where shadows creep
across the moonlight
many years away
beyond the long night
of endless alternation
rising in reverse
to fall and turn again.

And who are they
existing not
across the moonlight
shadows creeping?

Only in nightmares
have I seen them
intermittently appearing
indistinctly disappearing.

Remember to forget
that you came later
on a different plane
to keep a certain meeting
with the Fates.
Do not recall
what memory obliterates.

Predestined rendez-vous.
Arrival
by an unexpected route,
reaching at a separate time
the same
place unremembered
in another style and name.

Remember to forget
that you were here
before you came again.
The Fates debate.
The meeting is protracted.
Coincident
existence re-enacted.

Everything passes along
turning into different shapes
changes into something else
like a long procession
winding towards the distance

whereto wherefrom who dares
to say those here again
were not back there before
and those who were not
will not know they were

the whence they came
nor whither going
the something different
makes no difference
disappearing aftermath.

Those who leave
do not depart

ignoring each distance
along the pathway

those who remain
do not stay

listening to the sound
of footsteps receding

those who return
do not come back

expecting the unexpected
without finality

but those
who were not
and meanwhile
never were

unwittingly ignore
the dilemma
and escape
the confrontation.

We shall have seen
things yet to be
that were not meant
for us to see,

compelled to seek
from where we are
and peer into
the future far?

Or best forget
we then had seen
grotesque events
that will have been?

Tomorrow was
in days gone past
and not returning.
Times change.

Today foregone
that could not be
arriving now.
Time changes all.

And yesterday
will not have been
departing then.
Time-change.

These same three
by retrospection
juxtaposed.
Time concurrently.

Where does the road lead to,
the road we failed to find?
Perhaps it does not exist
and was obliterated
when the old highway
and the ancient crossroads
with the wooden signposts
were replaced by a motorway
and an elaborate exchanger
of complicated intersections.

We must have missed the exit
to the road we could not find
and shall we ever know
where it would lead to?

For us long since returning
there was no reply.

As you hurry along
trying to put as much ground
between you and your pursuer
as you possibly can
do not slow down
attempting to glance back
over your shoulder
or you will lose speed
and will not be able to see
what you would have seen
years gone time past
catching up on you
and will not have escaped
as you might otherwise
at the world's edge
the final elaboration

Life is rushing on
like a vehicle out of control
in the dusk without headlights
rattling and bumping
as it gains momentum
accelerates wildly
rushing towards the abyss
no means to stop
the surge forward . . .
nearer and nearer looms
the end of the ride
the inescapable conclusion . . .

Suddenly over the precipice
there is stillness without sound
into the dark silence
not falling not plunging
but carried along supported
on wings of quietness
by separate corridors
in time remembered
different ways dispersed . . .
to see the unbelievable
in life undying
by decease alive.

As you imagine
that I am here
when you are not

and as I think
that you exist
when I do not

if we are both
mere spectres
years away

how could we know
I *do* exist
and you *are* here

when this shall be
our non-existent
meeting place.

If I had lived that long
I would have told you why
it could not happen.

But as events turned out
there was no time to stay
and warn you wisely.

The rest were unprepared
while you spent time enough
in preparation.

You waited for the day
and pointed to the sky . . .
but nothing happened.

I once had thought the same
and might have stayed to hear
you argue further.

Though had I lived that long
I could have told you when
it would not happen.

On Fearing's Point
the landing stage
where tides unfurl
a sea green age

and coiling plants
in fathoms grown
re-navigate
the undertone

of sounding swirl
across the wake
of elements'
unfettered break

the landing stage
in green around
on Fearing's Point
the web is wound.

Drift downward in
a dreamless sleep.
Oblivion
close watch will keep.

Drift downward to
the ocean floor,
descending deeper
than before.

Tranquillity
will supervene
in that obscure
descent unseen.

Stillness opaque
where no wind blows.
Profundity
where no tide flows.

The time within,
the years between
are swept away
as if unseen.

The time within
which life forsook,
the years between
time overtook.

The time within
could not translate
the meaningless,
nor life create.

The time within,
turned inside out
the years between
the time without.

Sleep peacefully
sleep sound
soft easy sleep

before you see
the world
again resume

where you will be
away
receding now

so peacefully
in such
sound easy sleep

expressively
the last
who slept so fast.

The spirit world does not consist
of known confines in time or space
while spirits in a sense exist
they do not dwell in any place
they are not tramelled tangibly
nor do they move aloft in air
they have no substant entity
not here nor there nor anywhere
they congregate in nothingness
existence is for them upon
unmeasured spheres of emptiness
until they find oblivion.

When I am gone
you will not believe
that I have passed away.

When I am no longer here
you will not believe
(disbelieving
        the believable)
that I have gone for ever.

But instantly
you will believe
I shall return

a different way disguised,
you will believe
(believing
        the unbelievable)
that I am here again.

As I decided to return
descending from worlds away,
worlds of unreality,
to live again renewed
abiding in the actual world,
but now with hope of being saved,
let me recount what happened.

I lived just north
of Queenstown Road Station
for the whole of last year.
I heard every single train
out of Victoria and Waterloo
all day and all night,
even in my sleep.

But on Christmas Day
there were no trains;
the silence was unnerving
like the wilderness
at the end of creation
when Christ is born again
to save us from ourselves.

This is your Captain . . .
. . . . speaking . . . .
We are now approaching . . .
Civitas-Nova . . .

—But we left Finis-Terra
—only a few minutes ago.
—How can we have crossed
—the great ocean airborne
—over incredible distances
—in so short a time-span?

Fasten your seat belts . . . .
We are now ascending . . .

—We do not understand.
—Why do we not descend
—to reach our destination?

Because you will see
that Civitas-Nova
is a city in the Heavens
and we must fly upward
before we can land there.

You are not in this world,
but in the next . . . .
back to where you were . . .
back to where you came from . . .

APPREHENSIONS

"... STRANGE PRESENTIMENTS"

Amid the swirling of the winds
we sense
the working out
of strange presentiments
and with foreboding grope
to where it seems
our fate will be determined . . .
from shattered dreams
awoken by a sharp assault
to see
the substance of endeavour
frenziedly
cut down and trampled
on the wind-swept sands . . .
in disarray
from now forsaken lands
we hesitate . . .
barbarians drive us back
with all the resolution
to attack
and sweep viciously
across a landscape
changing unrecognised
into the wild shape
of anarchy
and whirling in our faces
sandstorms of despair
from desolate places.

To see the famous castle in summertime . .

(But do not go there
on winter nights)

I park the car . . we go in by the postern gate . .

(when the dead stand
on the broken battlements
watching and waiting
in the silence)

the way the castle was taken in the Barons' War . .

(they were betrayed
slain all of them
by treachery
the gate was opened
the besiegers stormed in
killing without mercy)

the sunlight fades . . we must leave now quickly . .

(the night wind gusts
then falls away
in dampness from the marshes
you would hear their shrieks
the silence is shattered
blood runs cold
as their cries are stifled
merging into nothingness.)

If you put the clock back
you will not see what you saw.
    Not to go back
    to where you never were.

If you put the clock forward
you will not get there in time.
    Not to go forward
    to where you will not be.

If you stop the clock now
you will stay where you are.
    Neither back nor forward
    getting nowhere in no-time.

A special consternation
is not far away.
Whatever plans you make
will come to nothing.

The Fates move against you
leaving you no choice.
Your hard won experience
becomes of no avail.

Not to have solved
every difficulty
is a reminder
of lost opportunity,

and if you think back
wondering what went wrong
you are likely to forget
what you might have learned,

stumbling along
where the road ends
in a rough track
of broken stones.

Any morning now
you may find
that you will not wake up;

any morning now
you may find
the incredible is happening,

your dream world
is tangible
and unreality is real.

You will probably never know
how it happened.

But if we are wrong
we should like you to come back
and tell us
what you have discovered
afterwards.

We shall await your report
with great interest
hoping to find out
whether you can prove us wrong
as we say again—

You will probably never know
how it happened.

Who are you?
Where do you come from?
In what sense
        is your inspiration?
Are you yourself
or someone else
existing
        in no clear translation
from undeciphered
ancient tongues
long since not heard
and such as can
be never read
                precise in word?
Untranslatable Etruscan?

Harsh realism—
the Law of Nature,
each living, struggling
organism filled
with enmity
to stay alive.
The world seen as
KILL or BE KILLED.

Behind the screen of
so-called "beauty"
and unaware of any
"love of nature",
without remorse
and without pity,
each sharply motivated
plant and creature,

fighting to
encompass what
is pre-determined
in the synechthry,
by poison, sting,
by tooth and claw
to KILL or BE KILLED
relentlessly.

By Saturn,
by the Sun and Moon—
these three,
Time and the Day,
the Tides,
a trinity,
and by the sequence—
Tiu, God of War,
Odin Overlord
and Thunder Thor,
and by our Lady Freyga—
Mars, Mercury
and Jove and Venus follow—
persuasively,
the Seven Rulers
by those Seven
swore
an oath
to keep the sequence
theretofore.

Do not buy that property
especially when if you do
you will have nightmares
and will see ghosts
on St. John's Eve
close to the cemetery
where skeletons rehearse
their dance for the Day of Wrath . . .

And here's another house
you mustn't buy . . .
the garden is next to woodland
near several special hospitals
housing psychiatric patients
who sometimes manage to escape
and wander about aimlessly
muttering to one another . . .

How would you like to hear
on a stormy winter's twilight
weird noises coming nearer
—wind in the trees—look there
—shapes moving in the darkness
—how would you like to see
creatures crowding round
faces pressed against the windows!

"These frightening dreams,"
the young girl cried,
"what do they mean?
  I wake in fear

  I dream I'm lost
and wandering
in forest dark
at night alone."

"Be still my child
  and rest awhile
  to save your strength,"
her Father said,

"I pray to God
that he may bring
you health renewed,
lest you go back

to sleep again
and wake no more
in forest dark
at night alone."

We climb too high
we are
reality away
from sight too far.

The sun recedes
and mist
blots out the mountain slope
where pathways twist

by dangerous
descent,
sheer the cliff edge neither
circumvent.

Lord o' the sun,
see how that Lord
radiates,
and afterward . . .

as he departs
we shall forget
what happens when
the Sun has set,

and if he were
as he were not
describing clearly
which was what,

then would you be
the same until
you stay no longer
as you will,

and be concerned
to reason why
no-one came
to say goodbye.

He told me in a choking voice
all his friends had passed away
so many years ago while he gets old
but they will never let him be
as frequently at dead of night
when he is lying weak and sleepless
they come back crowding round
he feels their presence closing in
although he cannot see them
he senses they would like to speak
but could not in their transient state
convey their changing attitude
with ever growing hint of menace
envious that he is living still
while they are as of nothing
and have no form nor substance
his friends are turning enemies
as they come crowding closer
and wait for him invisibly
while he is brooding on the past
their visitations now are sinister
his recollection more confused
infirm in body ill in mind
he does not wish to live
yet clings persistently to life
dreading the onset of each night
and what he soon will fear to find
the other side of darkness.

When I see myself reflected
in the long mirror
I am struck by sudden alarm
because there is always
someone standing behind me
reflected in the background
apprehensively I turn and look
but nobody is there.

Who is this creature
of which I can see
only the reflection
standing in the shadow?
Is it a man or a woman
or someone from another world?
Is it the tempter or the temptress?
Why does it not stay and face me?

I wanted to smash the mirror
but I did not dare
the omens were unpropitious
so I covered up the mirror
hoping even to avoid
the shadowy figure
lurking behind me
yet I fear to see it again.

It must be Autumn
leaves turning yellow
a chill in the air
as the light fades
in the short evening
across the valley
mist is forming
fingers of mist
like the fingers of ghosts
clutching at old remembrances
in the valley of twilight
merging into nightfall
the mist swirls closer
groping toward the windows
of the deserted house
the room seems to be the same
as when I was last here
if I can see the outline
barely discernible now
against the shadows on the wall
I expected to hear someone coming
footsteps on the path outside
are you trying to open the door
do not switch on the lights
do not disturb the shadows
surely I am not mistaken
there must be somebody lurking
in the obscurity of the night
shrouded by the white mist
pressing at the window panes
I shall remain here unobserved
not even daring to breathe
I shall stay by myself quietly
alone—in the darkness—
waiting . . .

Gratified that so many people
were able to attend my funeral
I regretted I could speak
to only a very few of them.
The time seemed too short.
Perhaps I was not quick enough.
In the circumstances how curious
to be the centre of attraction,
a kind of negative success.

"You were alone," someone said,
"nobody came to your funeral,
  the ceremony was meaningless
  with nothing accounted for
in that obscure conclusion."
To this I can only answer
I had the opposite impression.

I must investigate thoroughly
and I shall have to see those
who were absent, reminding them
by visitation of their neglect.

I will follow them in the dark,
a shadow they cannot elude.
I will haunt them in nightmares,
in terrifying shapes,
an apparition's icy grasp,
a dead hand from the grave.

Yes, it will be enjoyable.
I look forward to seeing them.

A temple in the jungle overgrown
with giant yellow flowers . . .
come with me
inside the shrine,
a message carved,
if we
can read the meaning
on the sacred stone,
we shall together go
as if unknown
to solve the script in Devanagari
long since inscribed,
and knowing it is we
ourselves who now must venture
there alone
to read the Sanskrit
where the great star
sings out hypnotic music.
Listen!
Who
is waiting there
when time has not yet run
to reach the zero instantly
so far
remote in space,
and speak in secret to
the star Capella,
giant yellow sun?

The dolmen you are looking for . . . it's
there,
over there at the top of the windswept hill.
This huge ancient burial place was built
by people living ages long before.
The stones have stood . . .
                    six thousand years or more.

It has an influence to shape events,
the centre of a giant astronomical map
where measured megaliths stand sentinel . . .
The dead are present in mysterious ways
to count the seasons and sacrificial days.

Do not climb up to that forbidding hilltop
where natural laws are known to be upset
and stones shall move
                    from their accustomed places.
Defy the unseen force, and not survive.
The great capstone will bury you alive.

Do not go there . . .
                    on this one night of nights
waiting for dawn at the summer solstice.
The stranger smiled as if in disbelief.
"I'm not afraid," he said,
                    "I'll go . . . alone . . ."
Next day they found him . . .
                    crushed beneath the stone.

"Dolmen. Megalithic tomb with large stone laid on upright ones."
(Concise Oxford Dictionary)

La fête foraine
est arrivée ce soir,
la ville est pleine
de bruit, de l'allégresse.
Les gens s'amusent.

Mais moi, je me promène,
morose, pessimiste.
Les gens se moquent de moi.
Je les regarde
avec mépris, avec haine.

Andromède, proche,
tragique, solitaire,
enchainée au rocher dur,
la belle prisonnière.

Andromède, l'autre, loin,
écartée de notre terre
à plus de deux millions
d'années lumières.

Trois cent cinquante milliards
d'étoiles: disque dense
et large, Andromède
dans un autre sens.

Impossible pour nous
de franchir la distance;
difficile à comprendre
l'univers immense.

LA DEMOISELLE QUI PARLE D'UNE TRAGEDIE AMERE

Je garde le souvenir
de ce que je vais écrire,
la douleur
dans mon coeur.

Un fardeau lourd, immense,
je porte en pénitence,
l'effroi
qui pèse sur moi.

Tous le temps je pense
à Dieu dans ma souffrance,
moi, brisée,
toute epuisée.

À LUI je lève la voix,
hélas, IL ne recoit
que prières
insincères,

toutes les longues nuits,
malheureuses nuits,
sans cesse
dans ma tristesse.

Les fleurs du désespoir
étouffe tout mon espoir;
amavi
et peccavi.

Les fleurs se dessèchent, blêmes,
les jolies fleurs, que j'aime.
Elles meurent
d'amour, ces fleurs.

Et je suis près de mourir,
la mémoire de mes soupirs
m'accable,
insupportable.

En quittant ces lieux
je dirai adieu
à la honte
que je raconte.

Mortes, les fleurs du mal
d'un tel amour fatale.
Je pleure.
Maudites fleurs.